To Adi and Dev, may Lord Ram guide you always towards
right action and right conduct.
– Chitwan

To my mother, for introducing me to the Ramayana and
the personality of Sri Ram.
– Sarita

To my mother, for bringing Lord Ram's grace to my life.
– Aparajitha

MY FIRST PRAYER TO LORD RAM is published by AdiDev Press Pvt. Ltd.
Thapar House, 2nd Floor, 163 S.P. Mukherjee Road, Kolkata–700026, India
www.adidevpress.com
contact@adidevpress.com
ISBN: 978-81-958992-8-9

Text and Illustrations © AdiDev Press Pvt. Ltd. 2023
Text by Sarita Saraf and Chitwan Mittal
Illustrations by Aparajitha Vaasudev

Printed in India.

My first prayer to
Lord Ram

A translation of Tulsidas' prayer that kids can read, understand and enjoy

Chitwan Mittal ☼ Sarita Saraf

Aparajitha Vaasudev

Publisher's Note

Dear reader,

First, let me thank you for all the love and appreciation you showed to *My first Hanuman Chalisa*, our first book in this series. Your enthusiasm and support encouraged us to embark on the journey of creating the book you hold in your hands now.

This simple translation of Tulsidas' original prayer has been crafted especially for children to read and understand. It is accompanied by beautiful illustrations that bring Lord Ram and this beloved prayer to vivid life.

When I was young, I sang and memorised Tulsidas' prayers with my mother. These prayers thus became a part of the rich fabric of the culture that shaped me. I hope that this book will touch your lives and create powerful childhood memories for you too.

Chitwan Mittal
Founder, AdiDev Press

Preface

Ram is an avatar of Lord Vishnu.

He was born in the Raghu Dynasty to King Dashrath and Queen Kaushalya. Ram was the embodiment of right action. He was well-versed in both warfare and knowledge of spiritual texts. His body was beautiful and strong. He was beloved of his clan.

On the eve of his coronation, he was exiled for 14 years. His younger brother Lakshman and his wife Sita accompanied him to the forest. During his exile, Ram travelled extensively and battled many demons. At one point, Sita was kidnapped by a king named Ravan and taken to the land of Lanka. During his search for Sita, Ram met Hanuman in the Kishkinda forest. Together with Hanuman and a monkey army, Ram went to Lanka and defeated Ravan.

The day Ravan was defeated is celebrated as the festival of Dusshera, to mark the victory of good over evil. Twenty days later, when Ram returned to Ayodhya, it was a moonless night. The people of the city lit thousands of lamps to welcome Ram home again. This day is celebrated every year as Diwali, the festival of lights.

Lord Ram is worshipped even today for his sense of duty, kindness, fairness, heroism and his commitment to ethical action.

Tulsidas wrote this prayer more than 400 years ago in Awadhi, an older form of Hindi. Even today, this prayer remains a favourite all over the world.

O mind, worship the kind Lord Ram!

man ↝ bhaju ↝ ↝ kripaalu

श्री रामचन्द्र कृपालु भजुमन हरण भव भय दारुणं।

Shri Ram Chandra kripaalu bhajuman haran bhav bhaya daarunam.

haran ← daarunam ←

He is the **remover** of the **terrible** **fear** of the **cycle of birth and death.**

bhaya ↙ ↘ bhav

His eyes are like **newly bloomed lotuses.**

↳ nav kanj

नव कञ्ज लोचन कञ्ज मुख कर कञ्ज पद कञ्जारुणं॥१॥

Nav kanj lochan kanj mukh kar kanj pad kanjaarunam.

Look at his **lotus face**, **lotus hands** and **red lotus** feet!

↱ kanj mukha

↱ kar kanj

↳ kanjaarunam

He looks like **infinite cupids**.

↳ aganit ↳ kandarp

His **form** is **boundless**.

↳ chhavi ↳ amit

He is **beautiful** like **new**, **blue**,

↳ sundaram ↳ nav ↳ neel

rain-bearing clouds!

↳ neerad

कन्दर्प अगणित अमित छवि नव नील नीरद सुन्दरं।
Kandarp aganit amit chhavi nav neel neerad sundaram.

peeta ↗ pat ↗

His **yellow clothes**, shine like **lightning!**

↘ tadit

पट पीत मानहुँ तड़ित रुचि शुचि नौमि जनक सुतावरं॥२॥

Pat peet maanahu tadit ruchi shuchi naumi Janak sutaavaram.

↱shuchi   ↱ruchi
I bow to this **pure** and **pleasing**
husband of **Sita.***
↳varam   ↳Janak sutaa

*Sita is King Janak's daughter.

bhaju ↱

O mind, **worship**

this **brother of the needy.**

deen bandhu ↲

भजु दीनबन्धु दिनेश दानव दैत्य वंश निकन्दनं।

Bhaju deen bandhu dinesh daanav daitya vansh nikandanam.

He is **Lord of the Sun** ↱ dinesh

and the

destroyer of **demons**

nikandanam ↲ ↳ daitya

and **titan clans!**

↳ daanav ↳ vansh

aanand kand

He is a **treasure box of happiness** and a **child of the Raghu dynasty.**

Raghunand

रघुनन्द आनन्द कन्द कोसल चंद्र दशरथ नन्दनं॥३॥

Raghunand aanand kand kaushal chandr Dasharath nandanam.

↷ chandr   ↷ nandanam

This **moon-like** child is the **son** of King
Dasharatha and Queen Kaushalya.

↱ chaaru

Behold the **handsome** and

generous Lord Ram!

udaar ↲

↱ sira   ↱ mukut

On his **head** sits a **crown** and on

his ears are **hoops**.

↳ kundal

He wears a tilak on his forehead and

jewels on his **body**.

↳ vibhushanam   ↳ ang

सिर मुकुट कुंडल तिलक चारु उदार अङ्ग विभूषणां।
Sira mukut kundal tilak chaaru udaar ang vibhushanam.

aajaanu bhuj

The **long-armed** one,

holding his **bow**

dhar   chaap

and **arrow**,

shar

आजानु भुज शर चाप धर संग्राम जित खरदूषणं॥४॥

Aajaanu bhuj shar chaap dhar sangraam jit Khar-Dooshanam.

↱ sangraam

battled the demons Khar
and Dooshan and **won!**

↳ jit

iti ↱   vadati ↱

Thus, speaks Tulsi
to Lord Ram.

इति वदति तुलसीदास शंकर शेष मुनि मन रंजनं।

Iti vadati Tulsidaas Shankar Shesh muni man ranjanam.

ranjanam ⤵   ⤵ man

You are the **giver of joy** to the **hearts** of

Shiva, the serpent Shesh and **saints**.

Shankar ↩   ↪ muni

You are the **destroyer** of the
evil army of **desires.***

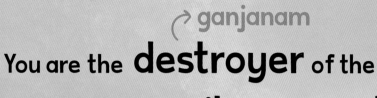

ganjanam

khaldal

kaamaadi

मम हृदय कुंज निवास कुरु कामादि खलदल गंजनं॥४॥
Mam hridaya kunj nivaas kuru kaamaadi khaldal ganjanam.

May You **live in** my **lotus-heart**

↱ nivaas kuru ↱ hridaya kunj

forever and ever.

*These include: desires, anger, greed, attachment and others.

Chitwan Mittal is a passionate educationist. She is the author of *Education of the Complete Person*, a book about holistic education. In addition, she has written several children's books focused on value education and bilingual learning. Chitwan founded AdiDev Press with a vision to create high quality children's books that would represent South Asian culture and values. She lives in Singapore with her husband and two sons, a constant source of creative inspiration.

Santa Saraf is a writer and an artist with an intense passion for reading, especially spiritual philosophy. She is the author of three monographs in English: *Nachiketas, Socrates* and *Abraham Lincoln,* and *Rahasyamaya Agni ke prati sukta,* a Hindi translation of Sri Aurobindo's hymns to Agni. She is currently in the process of translating *The Mother's Agenda,* a 13-volume chronicle of physical transformation. Value-oriented stories for children is another avenue which has been very dear and her first story emerged as a birthday greeting to her daughter. She now loves writing in verse.

Aparajitha Vaasudev is an illustrator, art director, graphic designer and dancer who loves creating beauty in whatever medium she is working in. She loves the challenge of taking a project and transforming it into something that adds beauty and joy to the world and meaning to the viewer, something that elevates and inspires. She is an ardent devotee of art in all its forms, and has unwavering faith in its potential to make a better world.

She lives in Bangalore with her husband, two cats and a dog.